Facts About the Gorilla (Western Lowland)

By Lisa Strattin

© 2016 Lisa Strattin

Revised 2022 © Lisa Strattin

FREE BOOK

FREE FOR ALL SUBSCRIBERS

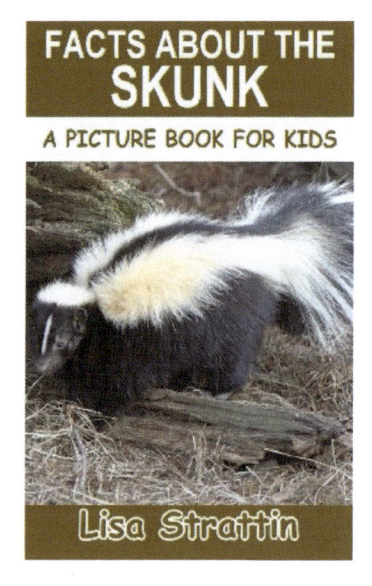

FACTS ABOUT THE SKUNK

A PICTURE BOOK FOR KIDS

Lisa Strattin

LisaStrattin.com/Subscribe-Here

BOX SET

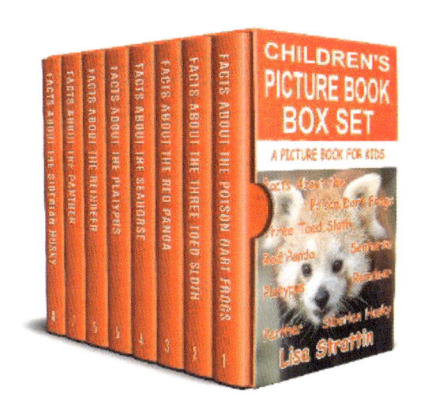

- **FACTS ABOUT THE POISON DART FROGS**
- **FACTS ABOUT THE THREE TOED SLOTH**
  - **FACTS ABOUT THE RED PANDA**
  - **FACTS ABOUT THE SEAHORSE**
  - **FACTS ABOUT THE PLATYPUS**
  - **FACTS ABOUT THE REINDEER**
  - **FACTS ABOUT THE PANTHER**
- **FACTS ABOUT THE SIBERIAN HUSKY**

LisaStrattin.com/BookBundle

Facts for Kids Picture Books by Lisa Strattin

Little Blue Penguin, Vol 92

Chipmunk, Vol 5

Frilled Lizard, Vol 39

Blue and Gold Macaw, Vol 13

Poison Dart Frogs, Vol 50

Blue Tarantula, Vol 115

African Elephants, Vol 8

Amur Leopard, Vol 89

Sabre Tooth Tiger, Vol 167

Baboon, Vol 174

Sign Up for New Release Emails Here

LisaStrattin.com/subscribe-here

All rights reserved. No part of this book may be reproduced by any means whatsoever without the written permission from the author, except brief portions quoted for purpose of review.

All information in this book has been carefully researched and checked for factual accuracy. However, the author and publisher makes no warranty, express or implied, that the information contained herein is appropriate for every individual, situation or purpose and assume no responsibility for errors or omissions. The reader assumes the risk and full responsibility for all actions, and the author will not be held responsible for any loss or damage, whether consequential, incidental, special or otherwise, that may result from the information presented in this book.

All images are free for use or purchased from stock photo sites or royalty free for commercial use.

Some coloring pages might be of the general species due to lack of available images.

I have relied on my own observations as well as many different sources for this book and I have done my best to check facts and give credit where it is due. In the event that any material is used without proper permission, please contact me so that the oversight can be corrected.

★★COVER IMAGE★★

https://www.flickr.com/photos/15016964@N02/3758756842/

★★ADDITIONAL IMAGES★★

https://www.flickr.com/photos/zooeurope/24563088855/

https://www.flickr.com/photos/poplinre/572816900/

https://www.flickr.com/photos/eileenmak/3615821756/

https://www.flickr.com/photos/47847725@N04/4530704187/

https://www.flickr.com/photos/mrfraley/46809330774/

https://www.flickr.com/photos/15016964@N02/3758876494/

https://www.flickr.com/photos/47847725@N04/4530705035/

https://www.flickr.com/photos/36107339@N03/46510488914/

https://www.flickr.com/photos/36107339@N03/40269001893/

https://www.flickr.com/photos/96541566@N06/51766414571/

Contents

- INTRODUCTION 9
- CHARACTERISTICS 11
- DIET 13
- LIFE STAGES 15
- LIFE SPAN 23
- SIZE 25
- FRIENDS AND ENEMIES 27

INTRODUCTION

Western Lowland Gorillas are an endangered species. It is one of two species of the large ape group, but the population of this one is more than their near relatives, the Mountain Gorillas. These gorillas are found in the Maiombe Forest that covers a large tract of Cabinda, Democratic Republic of Congo and Republic of Congo. They have also been found in Ebo / Ndokbou (Cameroon) where their exact number is unknown.

They choose to live in heavy rain forests. They also have shorter hair and longer arms than their Mountain Gorilla relatives.

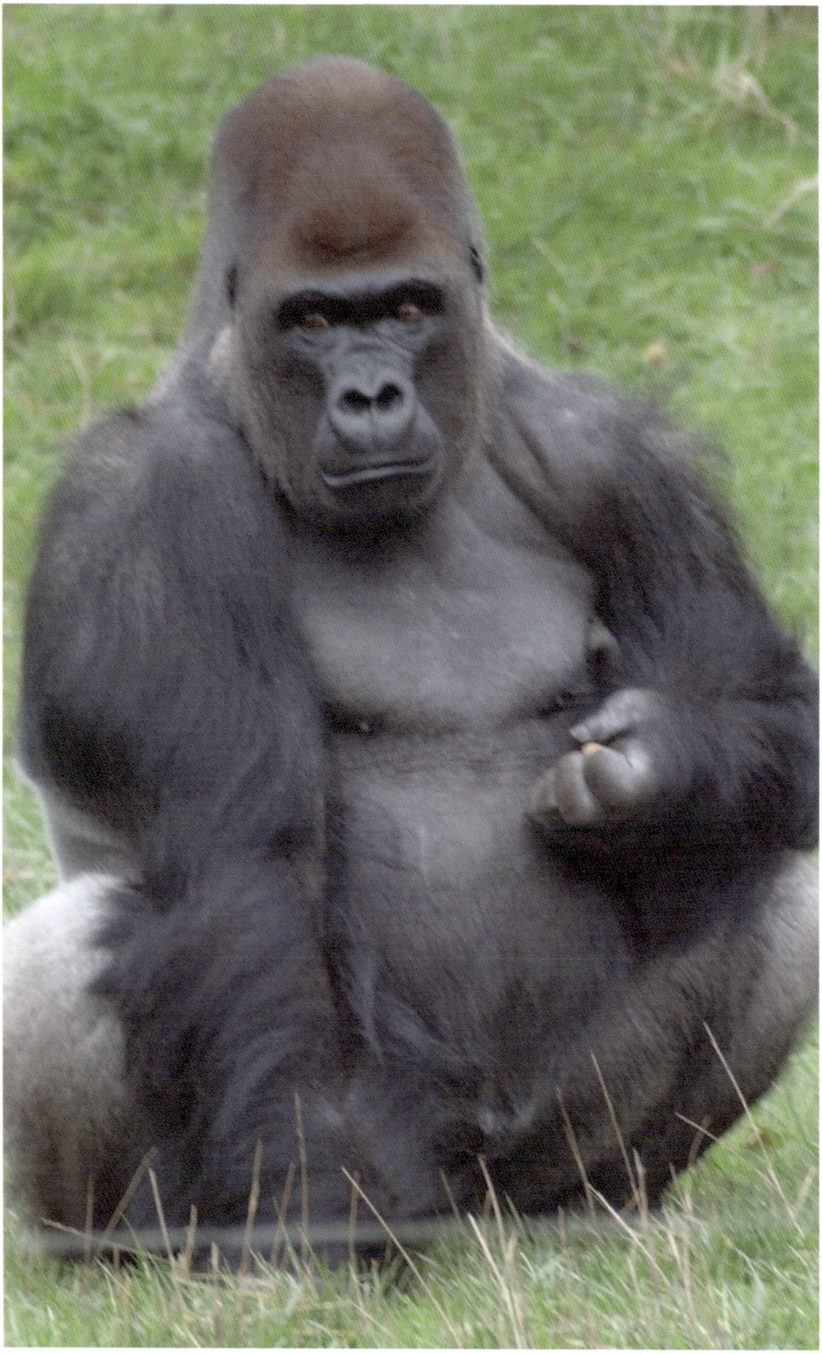

CHARACTERISTICS

These gorillas live around trees and can easily climb them. They do roam the ground in groups as large as thirty. Their groups are mostly led by one principal, aging adult male who is known as a silverback because of the ribbon of silver hair that beautifies his otherwise dark fur. This silver ribbon of hair displays its age and experience with the group. There can be a number of females in a group.

This one is the largest ape of all. Their shoulders are wide and broad, and they have a muscular neck. Their hands and feet are very strong. Their significant size allows them to defend themselves against any expected attack by predators. Their body is covered by short, thin grey-black or brown-black hair but not on its face. They do have a thick ridge of hair above their eyes very much like the eyebrows of human beings. They can cover short distances on two legs but prefer to get around by walking on all fours, using their knuckles.

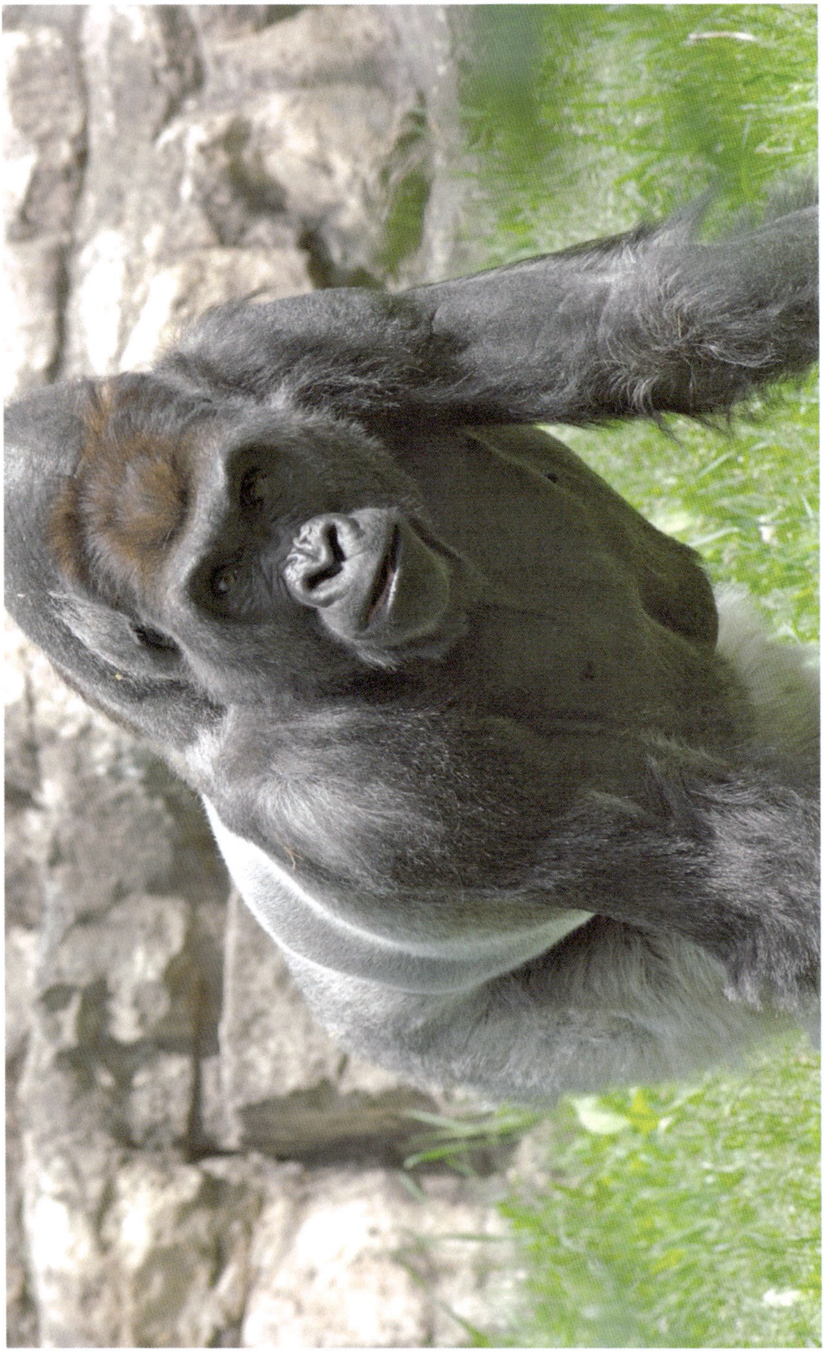

DIET

They eat both meat and plants but are occasionally classified as herbivores because they do love to eat plants a lot! They enjoy fruits, leaves, and shrubbery. They will sometimes supplement their diets with insects such as termites and ants. They usually do not drink water because they are able to get enough moisture from the foliage they consume.

About 2/3 of their diet is fruit, some seeds, leaves, stems etc. The rest of their diet includes insects, including termites, caterpillars, and other insect larvae. They eat fruits during the rainy season and feed on herbs and tree bark in the dry season.

When fed in captivity they preferred vegetables, fruits, and leaves. An adult male gorilla eats about 60 – 70 pounds of food per day but the adult female gorillas eat less than that.

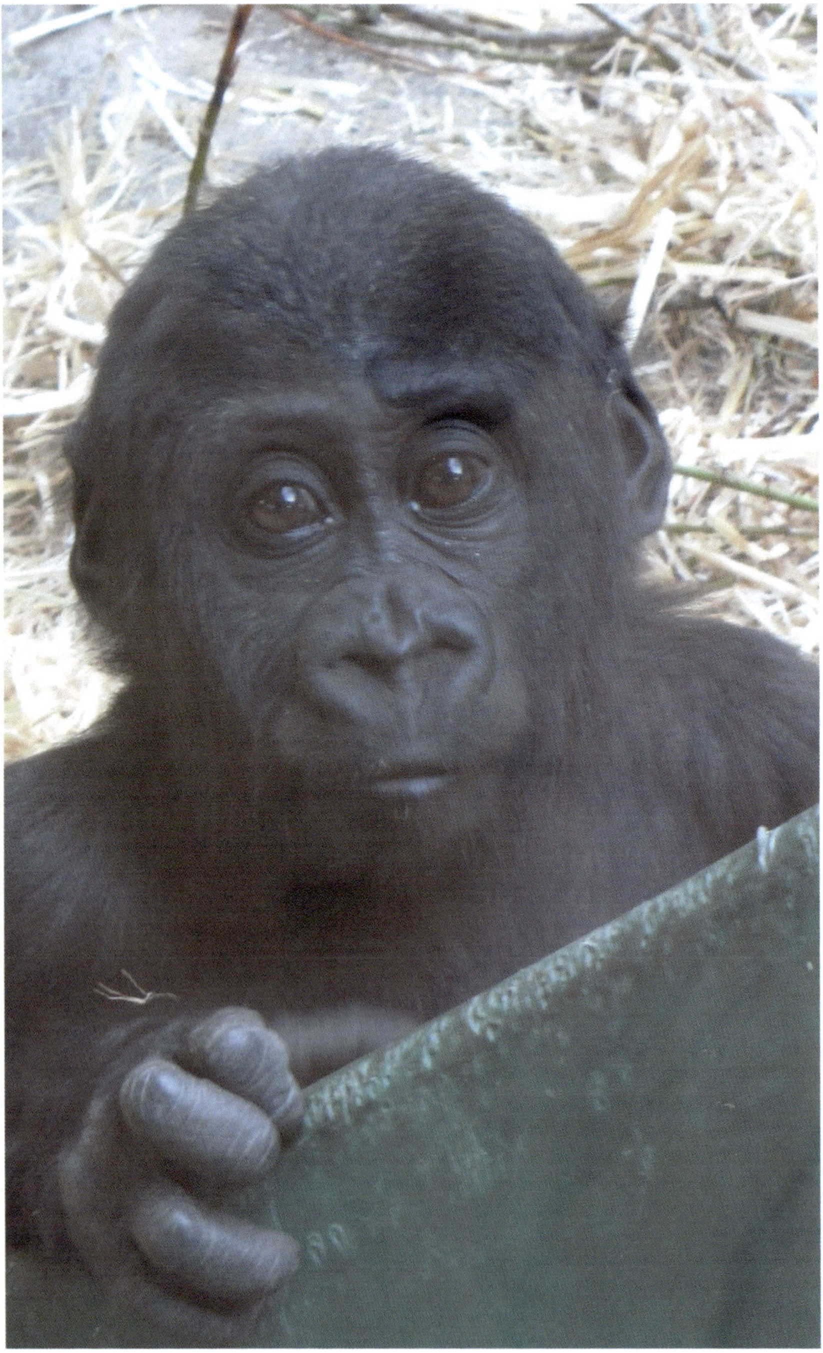

LIFE STAGES

A gorilla becomes mature enough to have a family between the ages of 7 to 8 years old in the wild; but in captivity it can start a family at about 5 and 1/2 years old. The gestation period of a female is from eight to nine months. Usually, they give birth to a single baby gorilla each time. After the delivery of the baby gorilla, the mother gorilla cuts the umbilical cord herself.

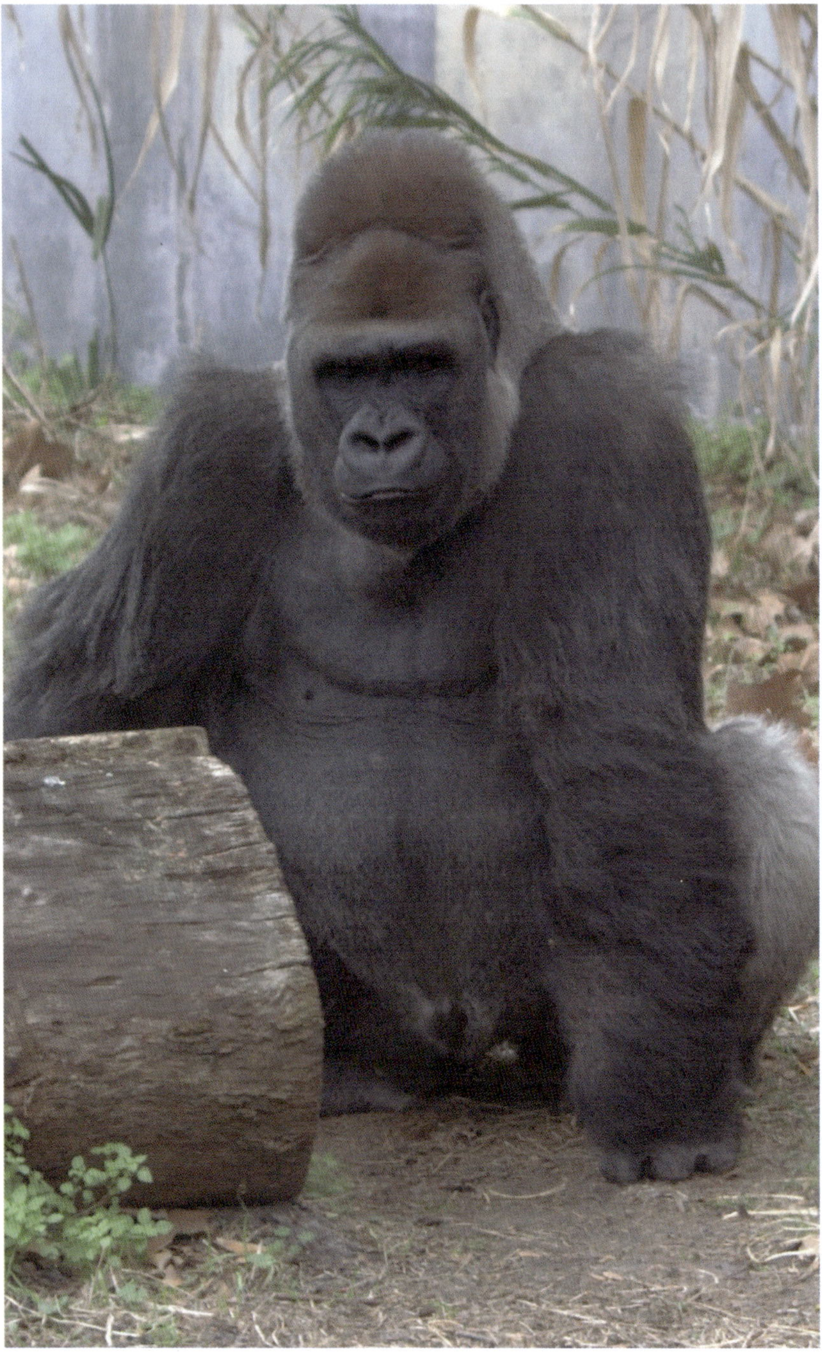

At the time of birth, their babies weigh around 3 – 5 pounds and have light hair covering their pink-grey skin. The mother gorilla embraces her infant belly-to-belly for close contact until it gets strong enough to hang onto her hair at about 2 months old.

A father who is usually a silverback takes on the role of a patient father and plays with the baby once it grows into a "toddler" age baby. Their babies begin crawling at about 9-10 weeks old.

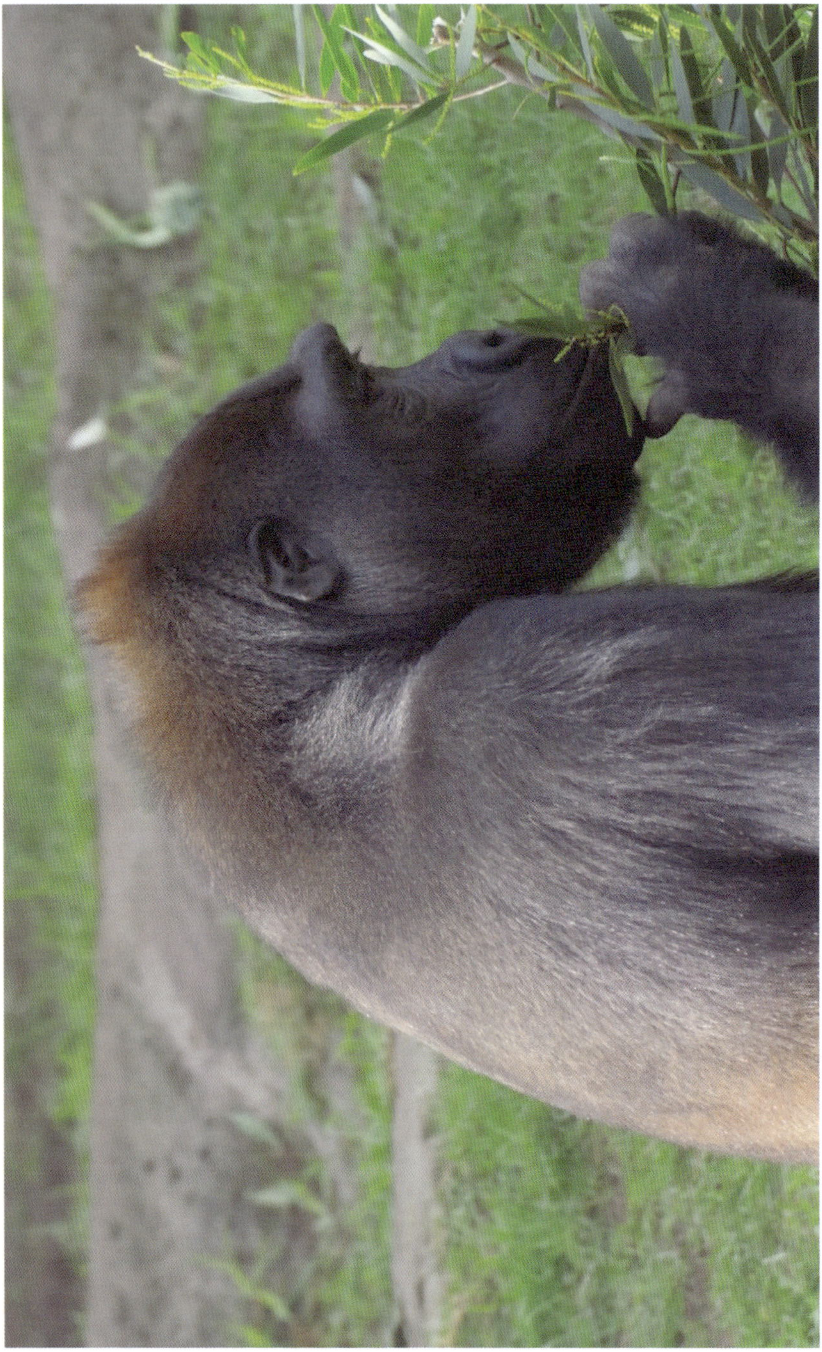

The white patch on the body of the baby helps the mother to keep a track of it and also lets other group members recognize the fact that it is a baby. This rear patch begins to vanish at about three years of age. Weaning is also done by mother at this stage.

Females leave the group when they get to be about 8 or 9 years old; afterwards they join a new group of gorillas or a lonely male. Males stay with their natural group until they are about 12 years old. They start leaving the group whenever they want to.

Solitary males attempt to get the attention of females from other groups in order to form their own group.

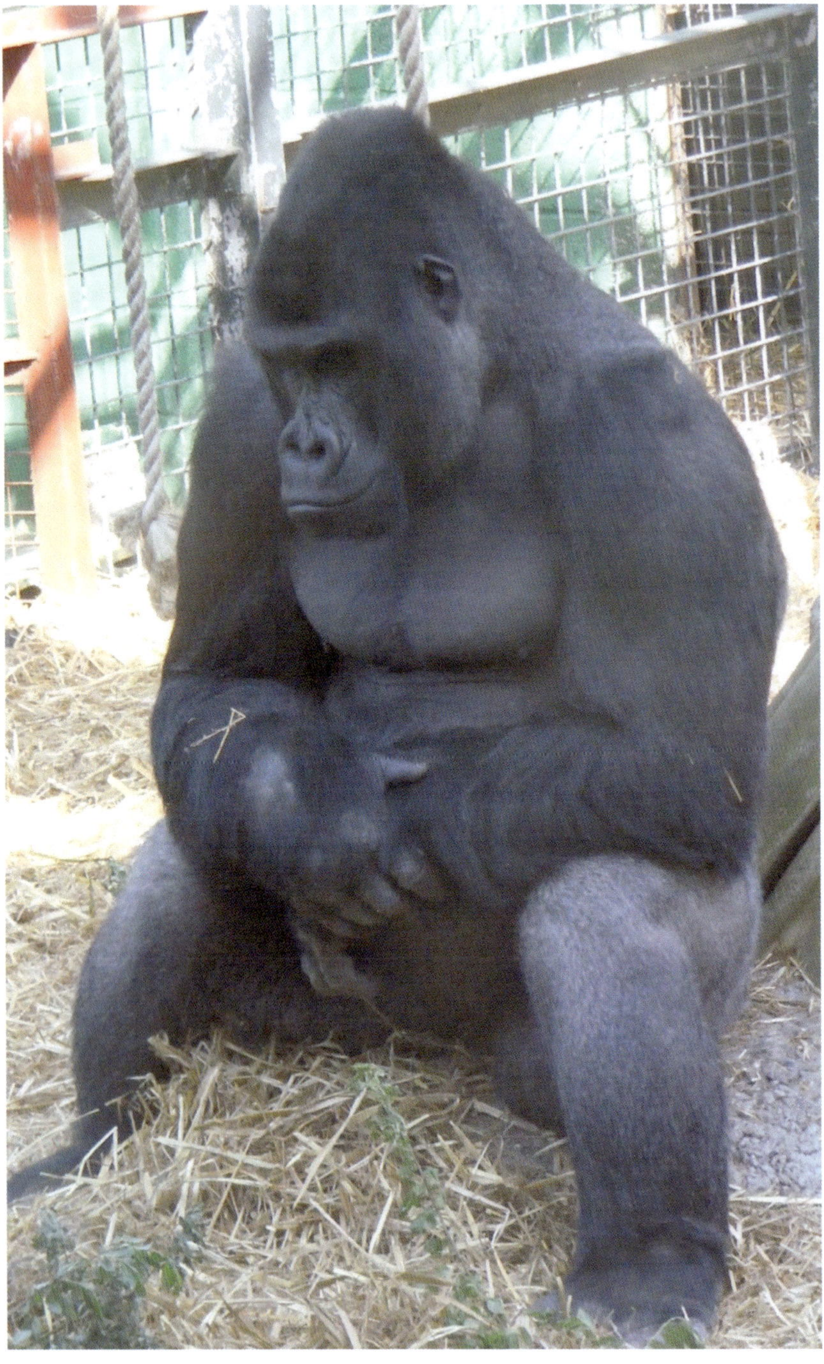

Only the silverback, or leading male, is allowed to mate with the adult females in a group. The success of males to find mates depends upon the protection of exclusive rights of the adult females, which is brought about by males forming an undying bond with each and every female in a social group. The formation of these bonds keeps adult females from leaving the group or breeding with other males.

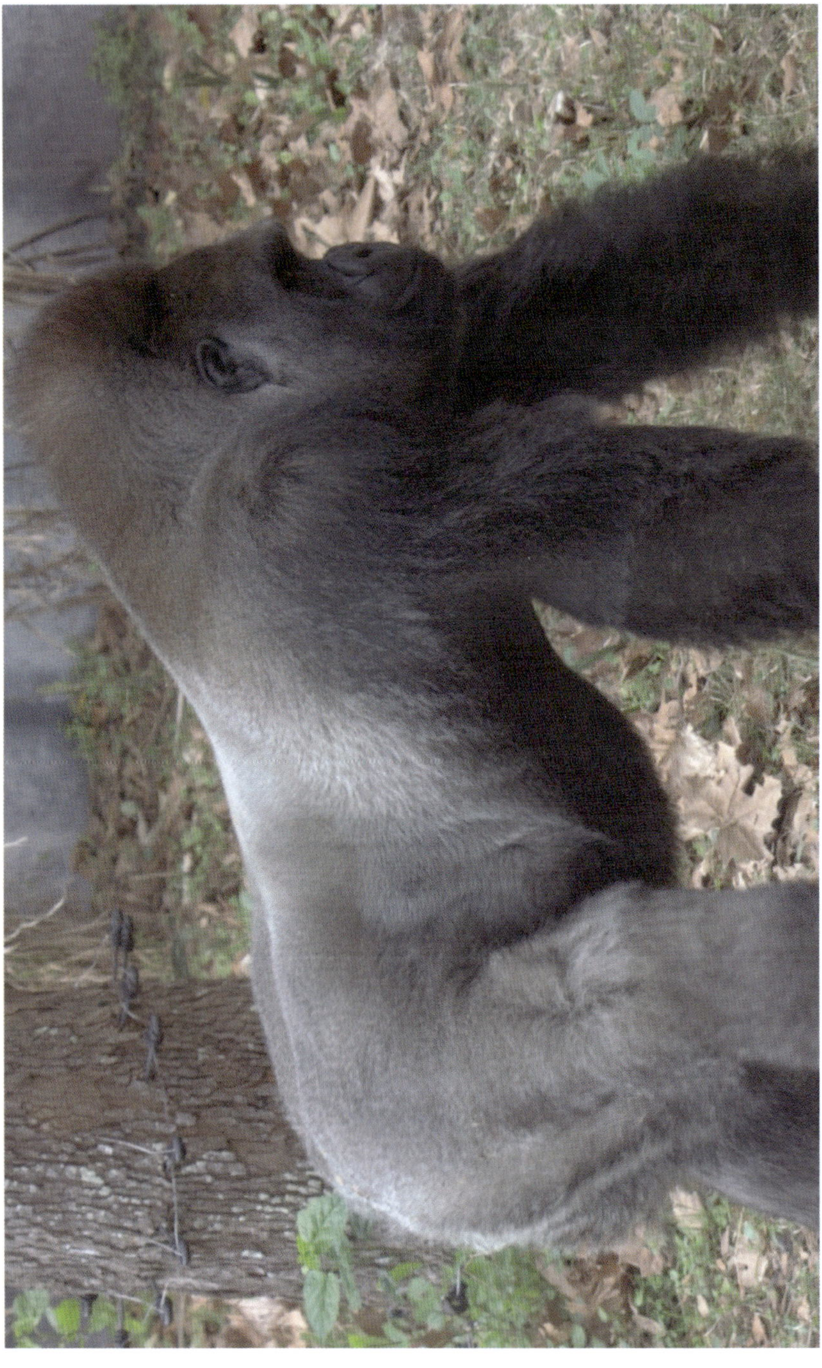

LIFE SPAN

Western Lowland Gorillas live around 30 to 40 years when reared in the wild and 40 to 60 years when kept in captivity.

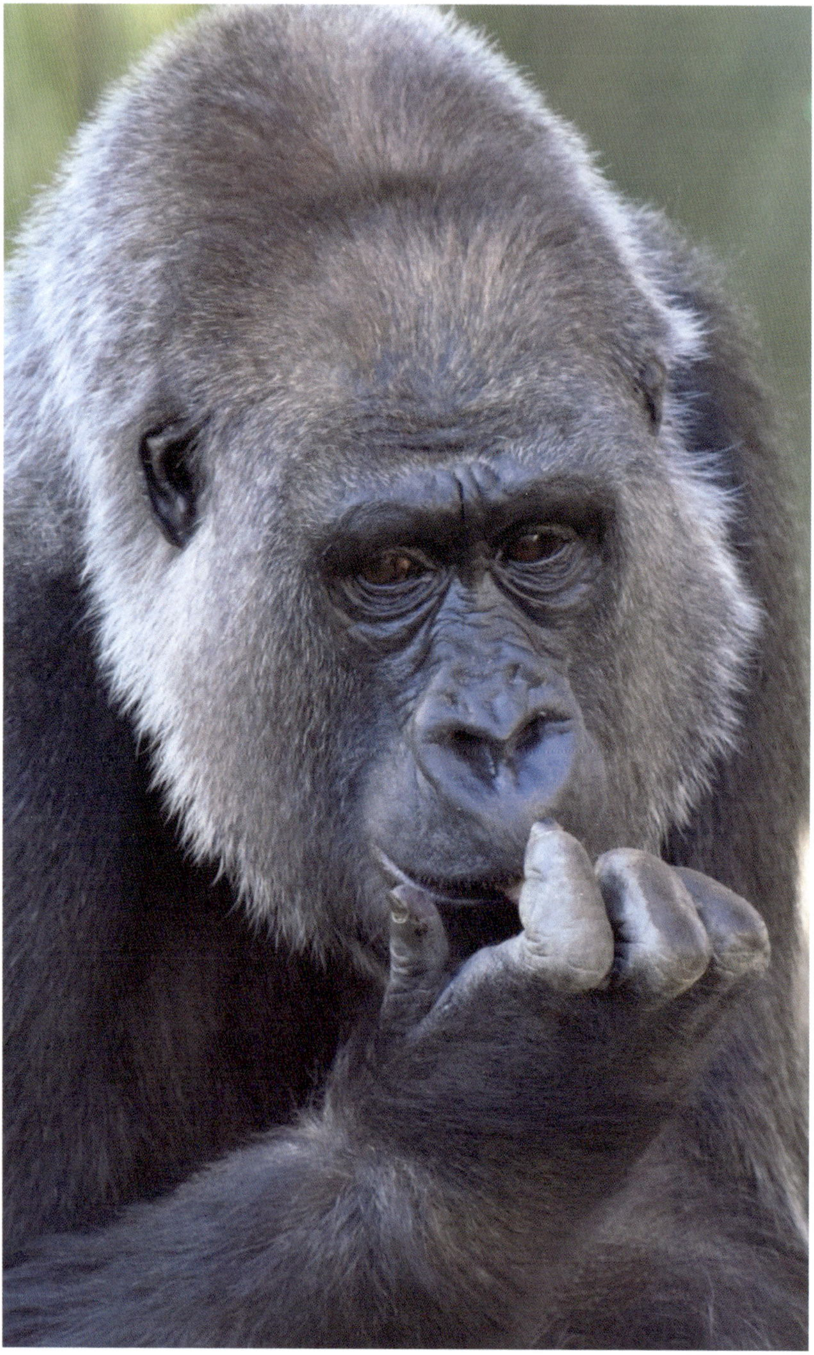

SIZE

The height of the males ranges from 5 to 5 1/2 feet and the females from 4 to 4 1/2 feet. An average male weighs around 350 to 400 pounds and a female weighs around 200 to 225 pounds.

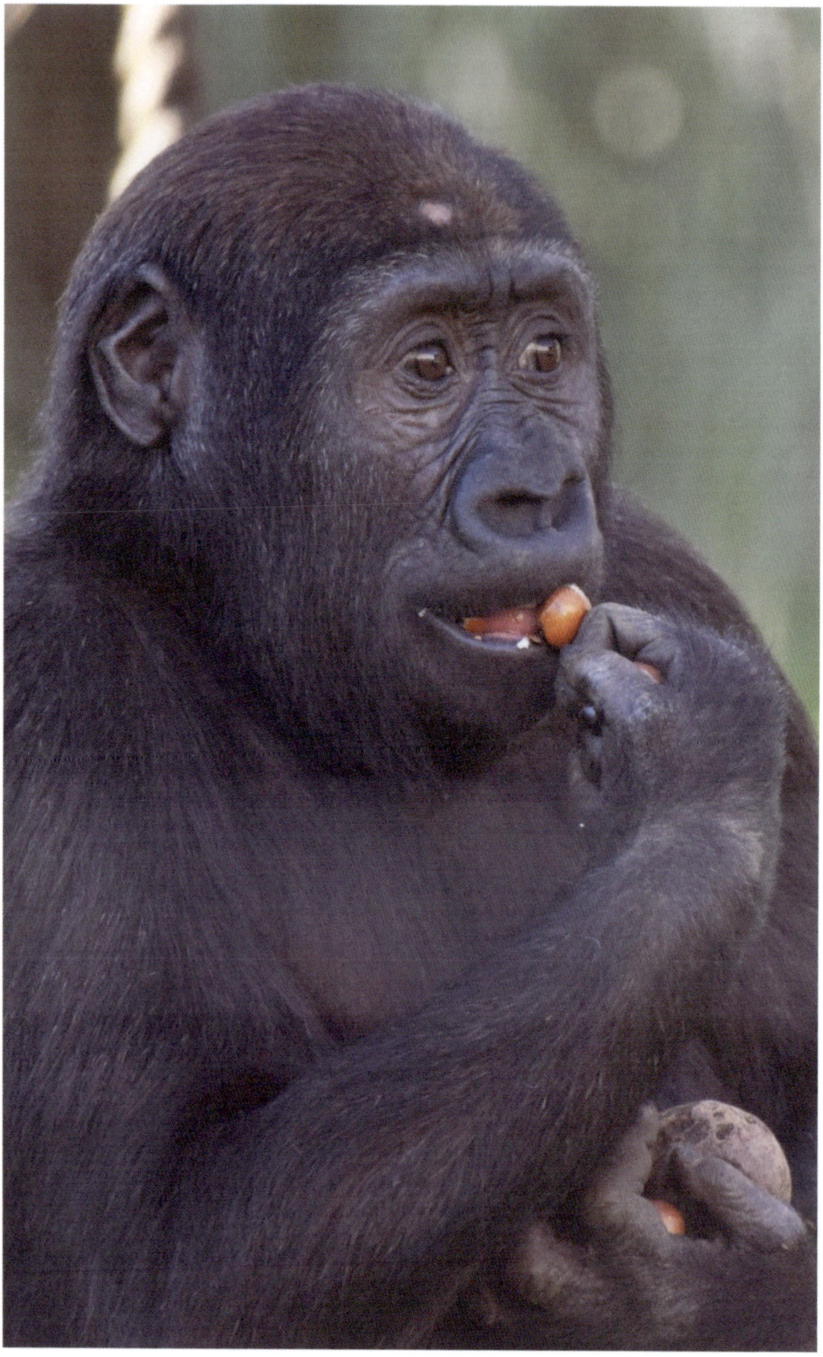

FRIENDS AND ENEMIES

These gorillas live in groups and become each other's friends. The most common potential killer to the Western Lowland Gorilla in their native habitat is the Leopard.

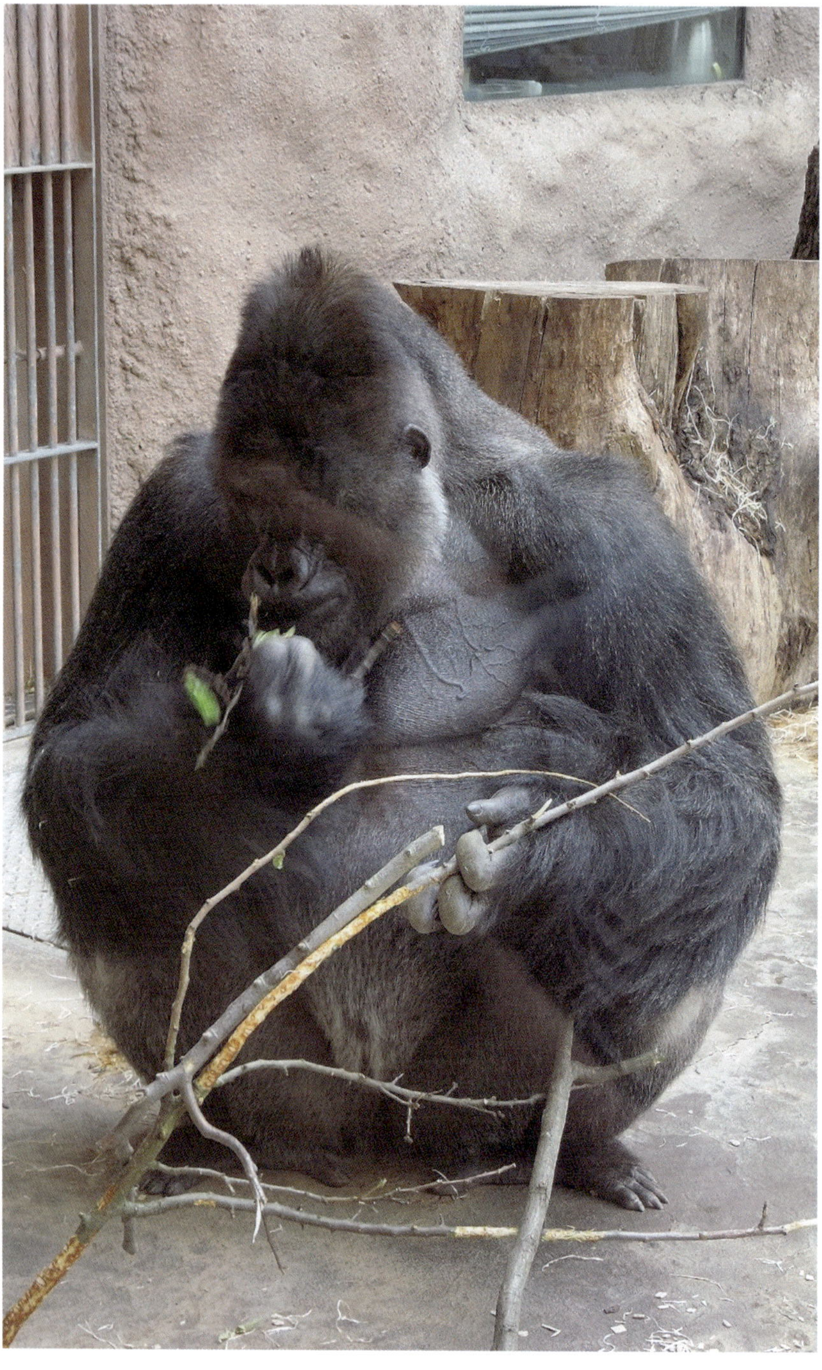

COLOR ME

COLOR ME

COLOR ME

COLOR ME

COLOR ME

COLOR ME

COLOR ME

COLOR ME

COLOR ME

COLOR ME

Please leave me a review here:

LisaStrattin.com/Review-Vol-171

For more Kindle Downloads Visit Lisa Strattin Author Page on Amazon Author Central

amazon.com/author/lisastrattin

To see upcoming titles, visit my website at LisaStrattin.com– most books available on Kindle!

LisaStrattin.com

FREE BOOK

FOR ALL SUBSCRIBERS – SIGN UP NOW

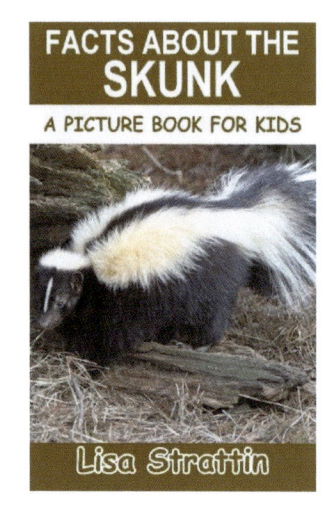

LisaStrattin.com/Subscribe-Here

LisaStrattin.com/Facebook

LisaStrattin.com/Youtube

Printed in Great Britain
by Amazon